Splash of Blue

a hundred poems you can fit in your pocket

Adrian Gutierrez

DEDICATION

For the underdogs, who hit back with brilliant knockouts.

ACKNOWLEDGMENTS

Thank you to the following people for making this book possible. Buster Jetter for designing the front cover and being available in a pinch. Diana Anderson-Tyler for the 'likes,' notes, and encouragement. Monty Holcomb for the editing feedback and arranging the order of the poems. And finally, Marty Rossi for your one-of-a-kind enthusiasm. You are all immeasurably talented!

if a mystery you seek
so you will find
if answers
well
that too
endless promise
can be discovered
in a book

one does not have to shout
to be heard
one only needs
to have passion
the more bold your dream
the clearer your voice to the world
you should instead
be loud with your life

the twine tangled
beneath every verse
the freedom of growing
in words you wrangled
your rigid mind steadily terse
rejects acceptance of knowing
answers to questions you ask

setting fire to bad memories
like burning sage
letting the smoke clear
coating the hard times

what will you do
with your regret
will you embrace uncertainty

can you turn your back
and walk away
from the hurt
you held
so close
to your chest
that pain that comforted you
when you were lost

any direction
even the wrong direction
seems better than none
because you know it's over
it has to be

you are too important
to let your past
control the spark
of your verve

what will you do

lost in hard times
i don't know what to do
sitting in silence
does nothing

asking for help seems pointless
so i continue fading
into sadness
alone

i wish i could
erase my memories
the ones with you
hurt too bad

i would happily forget
how i fell
head over heels
in love with you

when i brought you flowers
you threw them in my face
because you felt small

i pleaded with you
to take it easy
but you didn't

you yelled
and pushed me away
leaving a crater
of ruin
where hope once lived

i finally realized
there are some words
you just can't take back

dim lights and calm tones
of quiet nooks
appeal to me
without stillness
an uneasiness
stirs inside

there are too many rules
they create barriers
for making connections
and they keep me bottled

i don't like this
so i go to therapy

the weather has cooled down
a breeze gently blows through the window
i allow myself
to crawl into a relaxing space
which creates
a peace around me
following this moment
i sink deeper and dream

i heard
a fantastic story
of two latchkey children
who grew up
accustomed to instability
with no real chance
of amounting to much
at high risk of everything
when they became adults
and started living grown up lives
no matter what was thrown at them
each and every time
when they should have given up
accepting good enough
they didn't
they beat the odds

in a reflecting stream
your thoughts
clearly
betray you

the stories the bus stop can tell
about the determination of a woman
on her way to work
of the young man fighting the elements
while on his way to see his girlfriend
the state of the world
on any given day
will surprise you

you used my love
for you
against me
you refused to be
vulnerable

instead
you gave your fears
power

the same cascade of mirrors
drowning the sea of images
from the slip of smoke
against the tree limb
spars ever reaching
from mother to kin
a breath of life does us well

there is nothing scarier
than dreaming
of falling down
and never hitting the ground

i imagined the anxiety
was tiny lighting bolts
shooting out of every finger
directly into the floor

someone's prying freezes
my attention today
annoying me
like a bouncy fly
on my arm

the day is
the brook that dries up

tender moments
from the past have
gone away

what is left
is vacuous
a basin to hear echoes

i am the one who needs replenishing
then
the world can move again

you lashed out at me
when you were scared

steamrolling
my affection

then you hid
in your armor
of loneliness

the gravity
of death
is sad music

we hadn't talked in a few months
tonight when we did
it was fun
we talked about eating too much
and how bugs are annoying
we laughed at the crazy weather
and made fun of our social anxieties
we were really getting somewhere
remembering those long eternal times
when we were all that mattered to the other
then you told me you were pregnant
with another man's baby
it destroyed me

her flight settled in front of me
her focus on a hidden something
stare is all i could do
because she circled and danced around it
more interested i grew
at the edge of reveal i crept

she captured my attention fully unawares
in this moment i stuck
for the reason i can only justify
as curiosity
motionless i held and slowed
she looked up at me
and just as i knew i spoiled it

to the grass she bent
to pick up the worm

you are afraid of change
so you try and control
everything you can

while you do this
you hurt people
and lose friends

causing pain
that keeps you
awake at night

stop waiting and wishing
moaning and thinking
hurting and being angry
start going and moving
growing and doing
healing and forgiving
really
what is stopping you

if you miss me
tell me
because i'd tell you
that's what friends do

too much sun
makes me sink in
when shade is sparse
and retreat absconds

oh leaves of salvation
why are you so few

my lucidity circles flippantly
seeking desperately
for soothing relief
of a nice cool spot

when the entire outside has a fever
i count the calendar boxes
to a forecast of respite

please summer
break finally
and show me a season

your window to the world
is the only one where
you can actually see
the future
if you keep it clean
and keep it protected
it will show you a clear picture
forever

words and perception
inextricably linked
the danger
is understanding
why you
hang on
to the heavy ones

if you see me smiling
smile back
if you hear my laughing
laugh with me
if you feel my pain
we are connected
if you speak to me
i will respond
if you hug me
i will open my heart
if you love me
hang on to me

my young heart
left stranded
in piles of sticky sludge
waiting for the car to move
however
the wheels just spin

as i go nowhere
sitting in reverie
replaying our journey
waiting to be free

i will not remember
this lesson

when the roads are bad
i should just stay home

there is something respectable
about the wheels falling off
it's happened before
on this night though
i choose to ignore that notion
believing instead
that i'll have fun
and take the moments
as they come

furtively our souls came out
together we were learning to relax
the treasures of life
we shared and breathed
into each other
it was scary and fascinating
bravely we courted
and moved to that mythical place
coexisting with smothering zeal

sitting
watching a child
create a picture
is the most at peace
i have ever felt
the calm
in that beauty
is something incomparable
it is stick figured people
blue trees
two legged cats
and fat suns smiling
all of it poured out
effortlessly
by the purest gift
that exists

after months stuck in my head
feeling lost and sad
i made up my mind
to ask for help
so i went to
the doctor
she hustled me
in the office
sat me down
listened to my story
then she diagnosed me
with an attachment disorder

you can not control yourself
as i stand in your peripheral
and say 'hello beautiful'
it is not your knees that buckle
but the thick facade you built

my voice penetrates
deep inside your ears
while being barely audible
diving into your soul
forcing your entire system to attention

you are barely able to respond
as you weaken against me
'hey baby' you eek
trying to steady yourself
briery hairs saluting

i lean against you
just enough
for your body to feel me
and react
subtlety you press back
and smile
with your eyes closed
you open your heart

the foam on the coffee
told us so
it formed a heart

venerated in the melee
the weak rise up
and the strain
of tradition
crumbles

sleeping alone in my bed
every night is pain
endlessly running from fears
that i create

in my heart there is still innocence
there is no need
to feel so sad and empty
i am aces

you walk into the room
a smile you cannot fight
lights your face because you know
i am the one

you dreamed about it for so long
the tight shoulders melt away
excitement stays even when
life makes us weary

no more sleeping alone in our beds
healing rays delivered us
from hurtful thoughts
only love in hands as we hold each other

all we ever want
is the slightest peek
at what it is
to feel normal

while sitting under a tree
you accept your life
creating an impression
others see
and one
you can literally feel
like a slight chill
when the seasons change
there is a sensation
on your skin
the hair standing on end
bumpy textures signaling bite
the grand effect
causing delight

please don't scorn me
for seeing joy in solitude
i just need some time
to recharge

even on your worst day
after you had a sleepless night
with your mind reeling
from the endless thought

even if you don't deliver
your 100% absolute best
and it feels like you might panic
from shame and disappointment

even if all you can remember
in that moment
when you are overwhelmed
in the amount of work you have
and what remains undone
when time rushes away
in hands too big to hold
you must remember
above all else
you are still pretty awesome

colors in flowers
create sharp contrasts
to their backdrops

their petals enchanting
for a second look
urging and tantalizing
bright and beckoning

their elegance
pure and clear

a simple worker bee
i am
the pleasure of duty
in me
is to serve
my fellow bee

i extend my hands
into the clouds
as i propose the impossible
approaching the first step
with instant excitement

in your unconcern
for my feelings
you make me
feel licentious
for wanting you

i
then
became
my
own
martinet

eating broccoli starts out fine
you can roast it in a pan
or french it up with lime

fancy it any way you can
after it goes down
my inner highway goes on strike
as the timer begins

one day two days on
i suffer

the growling rumbling gremlin
screams and kicks at me
forcing my submission
before he finds peace
and my psyche relaxes
until the next time i forget
broccoli upsets my stomach

you deserve happiness
you deserve to be free of shame
you have the right to smile
you have the right to feel
you can trust people
you have to know
this is true

the hurt will not change
my purity
no seeping rage
no doubt will interfere

i have purpose
it is genuine

i am blessed with empathy
intuition strength and kindness

the open invitation
of presence
is quiet
and reserved

in it's subtlety
lies it's magic

my stalker has two legs
a hairy face
short extremities
the world through his eyes
is one big apple tree
with the sweetest reward
at the top

shiny
sparkly
treasures
are his obsession

days on end
of fretting
unsure of what to do
after i juggled the outcomes
many i could not predict
at last i chose
to let go
of the anguish

i have a new perspective
on what i do
when there is gossip
it makes me extra careful
who i include
in my life

i have a happiness about me
that no one else knows
it is calm and pure

what I see is the abundant silliness in life
without which we are miserable

and without this uniqueness
i cease to be me

some days it's blue outside
no one answers anything
so we force it
there is zero chance of happiness
and we plough through
some days the most beautiful visions guide
you
those days are great
relish them
because some days are the best
they are filled with smiles and laughter
some days it's easy to believe

instructions for me
include the following phrase
in every way
be happy

live to breathe
dream to love
laugh to enjoy

rejoice and give hugs
watch and grow
believe in happiness

you are going to be alright

instead of mourning
my childhood as a poor and sickly kid
with two ruptured eardrums
recurring tonsillitis
and countless other maladies

it is time i simply
acknowledge these facts
and not allow them
to sadden me

the best friend
i always had
was here all along

he has been waiting
for me
this whole time

welcome back buddy

desperate ripening
the channels of accretion
a meandering struggle

to move
and shove
through the pressure

a reorganizing
of energy
takes hold

as roots spread out
heat is created
momentum pushes
ever so delicate
this ire for survival

when there are
no other options
you finally submit

and through
the most indurate barriers
you break
as your tiny leaves grow

you put gifts in boxes
the surprises and secrets
you treasure the intent
there are many you have
right or wrong
big or small
safe
honest
secure
and the biggest one of all
there is only one box
the one you choose

home is a big deal to me now
it is the place
where i feel comfortable
and safe
i haven't had that in a while

my memory struggles
to identify a place
that holds the title of home
for me

home safe
home free
home run

home cuddle
home us
home happy

tonight was nice
the weather was pleasant
i had the company
of a friend

we drank hot chocolate
and attended
a church service
in a gym

afterward
we ate thai food
regaling the adventures
of the bad weather
and what would happen
if it trapped us in

instead of vengeance
i showed her that love can win
when i found my joy

when you feel afraid
know that you are safe with me
things will get better
i will always be there
to protect you

like a james joyce morning
you enchant me with excitement
your olive skin and deep kisses

floating on
the blackwood belvedere
lining the bath

glances in the mirror
steam fills the room

i pull you under me
to place my head
on your stomach
we lay together
and talk
into eternity

into the promise
of together
we drove

on the cusp
of forever

we loved each other
completely
in our passion we uncovered
a deep connection
with our honesty and openness
we grew close
during our time together
we found wonderful similarities

during the daytime
shadows move across the ground
in elegant shapes

they befriend your thoughts
reinforcing your theme
creating a silhouetted story

crispy greasy delicious
mom's frying up homemade donuts
they come from a can that
goes 'pop' when it opens
she says i can have
as many as i want
oh, there's icing too

tiny balls of fur
fuzzy little animals
their delicate nature
wraps
me
up
in thrilling pause
as i feel joy

i like holding hands
yours are magnetic to me
just a touch away

braveness is in you
you must never forget this
it is your birthright

on a small balcony
in the budding evening
there was a tiny sliver
of a crescent moon
a crisp in the air
the quiet
of a new week

on it i stood
contemplating everything
in a few quick seconds

then i thought
about a girl
challenging myself to this
what would i have
if i didn't expect the worst
and everything worked out
for the best

invite yourself to the conversation
you are welcome to the moment
stand up for your value
open your opinion for others
maybe someone else needs you
to make them a place
to feel wanted

cheering on those
who need a boost
you lend a kind word
in a moment when
you see their doubt

you pour encouragement
into them
as they find their strength

joyfully you become
the glint of hope
when they lose their way

the loud chaunt
of a winter storm
surprised me
with a whip and whirl
the angle of rain
suspended in sheets
wept against my awning

assured in belief
confident in thought
purposeful in action
clear in intent

courageous in all things
brave with yourself

composed when challenged
unafraid in conviction
peaceful to others
content with now

fixed in faith
cheerful in life

trust your intuition
your heart is delicate
don't be careless with it

i sweat when i sing
because
it is scary
to share
the deepest parts
of my romantic soul

ever so gently
i touch you
in the morning
as i leave for work
it is all for you

upon silence i sat
in isolation
wondering
am i safe

is it meant for me
to smile
when i walk outside

all day
i can imagine
being weightless

as i float around
to sounds
laid out by my angels

there is a vibrant trail
i found
in a concrete place
it was full of trees and flora
the path covered in wood chips
there was the sweetest smell
of nature
it must have been cared for
passionately

the crests of mountain peaks
draw me in
so different the scenery
from what i am accustomed
they seem purposefully
inviting

i am attracted to laughter
mine is big and moving
my body hunches
heaving
to express
the jubilance

drunk on merriment
i danced with a girl
in a parking lot
while friends applauded

then we stood
in the fantastic unknown

fate
daring us to try

there is little meaning
in the past
for you
it takes
no time
to show why

there is only
what happens
now

when you are young
you choose physical compatibility
over sense

when you mature
that changes
you prioritize instead
the warm appeal
of deep conversation

this time i wasn't torturing myself
the thought just appeared in a daydream
i was probably imagining
winning the lottery
or dating someone
who appreciates me

i fought the sadness
forced it to melancholy
then i squeezed more
to make it introspection

introspection i forged
into acceptance
and
acceptance
to
understanding

after all that work
i sat there
in reflection
motionless

i am thankful
for the serenity
of overcoming
a rough childhood

renewed hope
reinforces determination
that propels belief
free of pollutants

safely ingested
without harm
to anyone
this is destiny

through the leafy tree
a gust of windy air blows
singing peacefully

the rock remains still
through the turmoils of life
until we move it

there is a painting
made by a famous painter
that lives on a wall

it is tea time now
grab the cups and the tea pot
let us take a break

i sought a friendly conversation
from a shopkeeper today
he worked with concentration
in his skillful moves
the focus in his subject
deeply guided by sincerity
he solved and calculated
served and recommended
then sent me on my way

inside you
is the matching
cosmic dust
that attracts my soul
inside you
the energy
i need
every answer
to every mystery
i wander about
woolgathering
until i find you
my other half
my mirror
my whole enchilada

save one side of the bed for me
preferably
the one you're on

the plate is full
the house is warm
the clothes are clean
the spirit is energized

yet
there is still room for more

more peace
more kindness
more understanding
more giving
more affection
more love

ABOUT THE AUTHOR

Adrian grew up in a tiny town just west of Houston, TX. After high school he joined the military were he served in the U.S. and Germany. He earned a B.A. in Speech Communication from Southwest Texas State University, and M.Ed. from Wayland Baptist University. Working as a professional educator, he has taught every age and size of human from Pre-K to adults. His passions include writing, playing music, and CrossFitting.

Printed in Great Britain
by Amazon

16795269R00062